MW00436150

AN IDEAS INTO ACTION GUIDEBOOK

Return on Experience
Learning Leadership at Work

IDEAS INTO ACTION GUIDEBOOKS

Aimed at managers and executives who are concerned with their own and others' development, each guidebook in this series gives specific advice on how to complete a developmental task or solve a leadership problem.

LEAD CONTRIBUTOR	Jeffrey Yip
CONTRIBUTORS	Regina Eckert
	Cynthia D. McCauley
	Ellen Van Velsor
	Rola Ruohong Wei
	Meena Wilson

DIRECTOR OF ASSESSMENT, TOOLS, AND PUBLICATIONS	Sylvester Taylor
EDITOR	Peter Scisco
ASSOCIATE EDITOR	Karen Lewis
WRITER	Rebecca Garau
DESIGN AND LAYOUT	Joanne Ferguson, Clinton Press
CONTRIBUTING ARTISTS	Laura J. Gibson
	Chris Wilson, 29 & Company

CCL No. 446
ISBN No. 978-1-60491-073-5

CENTER FOR CREATIVE LEADERSHIP
WWW.CCL.ORG

AN IDEAS INTO ACTION GUIDEBOOK

Return on Experience

Learning Leadership at Work

Jeffrey Yip

Center for
Creative
Leadership®

This series of guidebooks draws on the practical knowledge that the Center for Creative Leadership (CCL®) has generated, since its inception in 1970, through its research and educational activity conducted in partnership with hundreds of thousands of managers and executives. Much of this knowledge is shared—in a way that is distinct from the typical university department, professional association, or consultancy. CCL is not simply a collection of individual experts, although the individual credentials of its staff are impressive; rather it is a community, with its members holding certain principles in common and working together to understand and generate practical responses to today's leadership and organizational challenges.

The purpose of the series is to provide managers with specific advice on how to complete a developmental task or solve a leadership challenge. In doing that, the series carries out CCL's mission to advance the understanding, practice, and development of leadership for the benefit of society worldwide. We think you will find the Ideas Into Action Guidebooks an important addition to your leadership toolkit.

Table of Contents

EXECUTIVE BRIEF

Leadership is best learned from experience, but learning from experience is not always automatic. This guidebook introduces you to a return-on-experience framework. Using this ROE framework, you actively seek to learn from experience in order to build your mastery, broaden your versatility, and benefit your organization. When you understand and apply the framework in your work and organization, everyday experiences can be transformed into an engine for leader development and organizational impact.

Experience as a Leadership Engine

Anna is a senior operations executive with an American manufacturing company. She recently completed a two-year expatriate assignment overseeing the transfer of production to a plant in Brazil. During that time, she increased her mastery of business negotiations and gained greater operational skill—areas in which she had previous skill and success.

Leading a production start-up in an unfamiliar country and culture also stretched Anna's leadership capacity. She learned to navigate regulatory and legal systems, build local partnerships, and operate within an unfamiliar culture. She managed a diverse senior team and juggled tensions between local realities and corporate directives.

Now, back in the U.S., she has found that the lessons she learned abroad are applicable in her new role as vice president of North American operations. She is more adept (and more confident) as she bridges strategic and operational demands across four locations. Anna's time in Brazil has influenced her leadership style and operational perspective, benefiting her team and her organization as a whole.

As Anna found, nothing teaches leadership like experience. CCL's global research on how leaders learn shows that a considerable amount of the learning that managers experience during their careers comes from dealing with the challenges of their work. But the benefits of that on-the-job learning opportunity are not guaranteed. To maximize the learning and development potential that lies within work experience, you need a plan. You need to understand what you are gaining from your experience, what is missing, and how to fill any gaps.

This guidebook introduces you to a return-on-experience framework. Using the ROE framework, you actively seek to learn from experience in order to develop your mastery, versatility, and

7

impact. You can use the ROE framework to guide your leadership development and also apply it in your organization to

- identify experiences that teach critical skills
- uncover leadership lessons from experience
- integrate experience with learning, and learning with impact
- create a portfolio to track and improve performance
- understand the role of learning from experience for your own career planning and development
- articulate the value of experience to others: bosses, superiors, potential new employers
- improve your ability to coach and develop others in your organization

Adopting an ROE mind-set is a powerful career strategy, especially in an era when the ability to learn and adapt is essential for surviving and succeeding in the workplace. When you understand and apply the ROE framework in your work and organization, everyday experiences can be transformed into an engine for leader development and organizational impact.

Build, Broaden, Benefit

As a leader, you know that much of your skill and learning has evolved through your work experience. CCL studies support this. The ability to learn is a key criterion that differentiates successful executives from those who derail. Ongoing on-the-job learning is an essential ingredient for long-term leadership success.

An ROE mind-set helps you strengthen your ability to learn, develop important skills, and—at the same time—do your work. Rather than assuming that your work will automatically teach you what you need to know, you can create a new learning habit that uses experience to build, broaden, and benefit.

Build. Experience-based learning can enhance mastery. The development goal is to increase your capability by sharpening your existing skills and ability to lead.

Broaden. Experience-based learning can enhance versatility. The development goal is to expand your repertoire of skills and abilities.

Benefit. Experience-based learning can enhance impact. The true measure of learning is your ability to apply it. To have value, learning must be transferable to different situations and to other people.

The build-broaden-benefit concept allows you to view work through a new lens. You will actively start to seek out experiences that teach, and learn more from the experiences that you are given. This approach to learning from experience—mastery plus versatility plus impact—is a new framework for many managers.

Often career and development strategies focus on either a higher level of expertise or cross-functional learning. The ROE framework connects the two. Mastery prepares managers for existing and identified challenges. Versatility prepares managers for new and potential unknown challenges—situations which may be different from ones they have already experienced.

The combination of mastery and versatility produces a "T-shaped leader"—someone who possesses high capabilities in a core function (the vertical part of the T) with broad capacities in diverse areas (the horizontal part of the T). See the figure on page 10. T-shaped leaders are well equipped to add the third element of ROE: impact. By reaching out into your group and organization, you can extend new skills and valuable knowledge, enhancing the impact of your learning and experience.

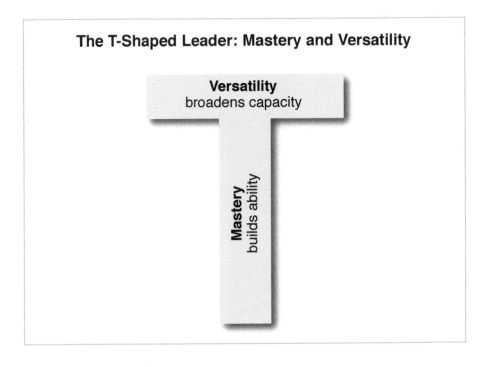

When going through an experience, you can ask yourself three key questions:

- What skills am I building?

- How can I broaden my perspective or extend my capability?

- How can my experiences and my increased mastery and versatility benefit my organization?

If your experiences fall short on developing mastery, versatility, or impact, the message is clear: it is time for a change. You will want to seek out new work and learning opportunities or rethink how you approach your current work.

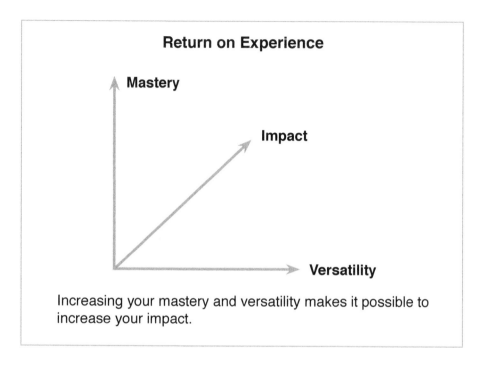

Return on Experience

Increasing your mastery and versatility makes it possible to increase your impact.

Build: Heighten Your Mastery

Mastery is a progressive process in which the lessons learned from experience build on each other. The development goal is to increase mastery by sharpening your existing skills and ability to lead.

In many technical arenas, mastery is fairly easy to gauge. Skill increases with the addition of training, experience, and time. For example, a software developer may seek out additional training, practice through hands-on projects, and gain confidence and skill through bigger assignments. Over time, she becomes highly skilled in her field.

Leadership expertise is similarly honed; however, it may be harder to know what you need to learn and how to go about learning it. For example, the ability to build and lead a team is a key leadership skill. Lena, a project manager for an energy consultancy, has worked in team-based environments her entire career. Her roles and responsibilities have changed over the years, and she defines herself as a team player and someone who collaborates well with others.

Lena is eyeing a move to a director-level job, in which she would have a role in hiring employees, assigning project teams,

---

Can You Be a Fox and a Hedgehog?

"The fox knows many things, but the hedgehog knows one big thing."

These are the words of the Greek poet Archilochus, made famous by the philosopher Isaiah Berlin. Berlin suggests that leaders can be divided into two categories: hedgehogs, who lead by expertise and mastery, and foxes, who are versatile in multiple areas but masters of none. Berlin's categorization is an interesting one. What type of leader is more capable of leading an organization through troubling times? The expert hedgehog or the versatile fox?

Jim Collins (2001) is an advocate of the hedgehog leader, writing:

> Those who built the good-to-great companies were, to one degree or another, hedgehogs. They used their hedgehog nature to drive toward what we came to call a Hedgehog Concept for their companies. Those who led the comparison companies tended to be foxes, never gaining the clarifying advantage of a Hedgehog Concept, being instead scattered, diffused, and inconsistent. (p. 92)

CCL's work shows that neither type of leader is ideal; there are clear strengths and trade-offs for each. Instead, organizations need leaders who are able to combine the laserlike mastery of the hedgehog with foxlike versatility and openness to possibilities.

and making strategic decisions based on input from the teams. The way she leads and works with teams will necessarily shift if she earns the promotion, and she wants to be prepared. How can she better understand team dynamics and her own leadership style so that she can build her capacity and confidence? Lena's situation is one that requires greater mastery. She wants to improve her ability to lead a team—fine-tuning her approach and building on her current skill.

To increase leadership mastery, the first step is to identify what needs to be learned or improved. You'll want to look at this from two perspectives: the needs of the organization and your own needs.

Needs of the Organization

Align your learning experiences with the needs of the organization. What are the strategic challenges and priorities the organization faces? What leadership skills does it need to meet those challenges?

When your developmental experiences are aligned to the strategic priorities of the organization, the skills that you develop from the experience go toward building leadership mastery in ways that have direct relevance to your career and a benefit to the organization in the long term. If, like Lena's, your organization requires sophisticated team-based leadership, then seek out assignments that develop those skills. If, instead, your organization operates along formal lines of authority, you might seek out assignments that help you improve your ability to make decisions, influence others, and negotiate.

Many organizations have competency frameworks that describe the types of leadership capabilities needed to do specific jobs and to achieve the work of the organization. If these skills are not explicit or sufficiently detailed, ask around. Talk to someone who has the kind of job you want in the future, ask your boss to describe what it would take for you to grow in the organization, and observe successful people and decipher their skills and behaviors.

Your Own Needs

Match developmental experiences to your needs. Customize your learning agenda based on your own strengths and development needs. An experience that may be developmental for you may not be useful or have the same effect on others. The process of developing mastery differs by individuals and the context of their work.

Consider two production managers, Omar and Michael. Both work in the same facility with equivalent roles and levels of responsibility. Omar was hired in from another industry, in which he gained operational skills as well as extensive people management skills. He routinely made hiring and firing decisions, conducted reviews, and coached direct reports. He is sharpening his skills in his current job, with a particular focus on coaching and development of those on his team.

Michael, a skilled employee, was promoted based on his technical know-how. In his prior role as a team leader, he had no role in managing personnel issues. Michael feels challenged by the human side of leading his department. His learning focus is on improving his ability to manage assignments, document performance, and give feedback.

Michael and Omar have similar roles, but they bring very different levels of mastery to the personnel aspects of their jobs. What they need to learn and the experiences they need are vastly different.

Strategies for Building Mastery

To heighten your skills, seek experiences that offer appropriate challenges that will stretch your capabilities. Strategies for building mastery include the following:

Strategic assignments. Go after tasks and roles that give you reason to practice the skills you need to learn. Identify specific capabilities or areas to develop, assess your current skill level, and use the work assignment as a lab for learning. Try new behaviors, practice new skills, ask for feedback, and reflect on your level of improvement. A strategic assignment might be something you give yourself, but you are more likely to arrange it through your boss or mentor.

On your own, you may set a goal to improve a specific behavior or build your skill through existing work and responsibilities. Or you could volunteer to add an assignment to your duties or take on a new initiative.

A more formal example comes from Cisco's Leadership Fellows Initiative. Through the program, Cisco employees have the opportunity to serve in one- to two-year volunteer assignments in nonprofit organizations. Each assignment is matched to the individual's professional expertise and the strategic priorities of Cisco. Through these experiences, employees hone and shape existing abilities in ways that they may not have in their existing on-the-job roles.

Job rotations. Similar to a strategic assignment, a job rotation gives you the chance to apply your skill set in a new context. Many people leave their departments to gain this experience, but job rotations within your department may be equally beneficial.

If your organization doesn't accommodate rotations, seek out ways to learn other functions or areas of the business. For example, you could cover for a colleague on maternity leave—giving you new experience while filling an organizational need. Or you could trade tasks with a peer: offer to prepare and give the monthly sales presentation in exchange for one of your routine assignments. Institute a process of rotating roles within your team as a developmental opportunity for everyone.

Action learning projects. These assignments marry individual developmental experiences to the strategic priorities of the organization. The goal of an action learning project is to address a pressing business problem while expressly learning through the experience.

For example, at GE, the action learning process requires managers to contribute ideas to build the business and then work in teams to implement the ideas. Typically, two teams of five to seven people from diverse businesses and functions within GE work together on the problem. They build in time for learning, with the team members reflecting on the process and the experience. As a result, the managers develop a broader perspective about the organization and acquire strategic and operational skills grounded in the context of their organization.

Broaden: Increase Your Versatility

Whereas mastery represents a move toward more expertise, versatility represents a move toward breadth of capacity. It is about the expansion of your capacity through learning. When you learn new skills or gain new perspectives from experience, you can extend the arena of possibilities within which they operate and open up new repertoires of thinking and acting. You are able to break reinforcing cycles of unproductive beliefs and behaviors by exposure to experiences that challenge your current ways of thinking.

Max has moved up the ranks from team member to group leader to department manager. He was recently tapped to manage a cross-functional, cross-location team charged with responding to a widespread quality problem. Max knows he's been an effective leader in the past, but working with a diverse, dispersed, often territorial group of people will introduce him to new, significant challenges.

Max knows this assignment is a critical one. The stakes are high, and his boss is looking to see whether Max has what it takes. The role is also a pivotal learning opportunity for him.

A variety of developmental experiences can lead to an increased repertoire of management skills necessary to function effectively in global organizations. Different types of assign-  ments—such as new initiatives, fix-its, and working in a different culture—contribute essential but different lessons.

Strategies for Broadening Versatility

Seek experiences that will expand your repertoire of skills and abilities. Strategies for broadening versatility include the following:

Go vertical. What assignments require you to work across organizational boundaries of level and hierarchy? Examples include supervisory responsibility, mentoring roles, managerial responsibilities with hierarchical reporting relationships, and special assignments with senior executives.

Reach across. Horizontal assignments require managers to work across organizational boundaries of function and expertise. Examples include job rotations, working on a cross-functional team, and action learning projects involving different subject matter experts.

Engage with outsiders. Stakeholder assignments require managers to work across the boundaries of the firm, to interface with stakeholders. Examples include managing joint ventures, working with vendors, and being responsible for public affairs or corporate citizenship functions.

Cross geographic boundaries. Assignments that require managers to work across geographically defined boundaries of regions and nations also enhance versatility. Examples include international assignments, regional or global management responsibilities, and management of geographically dispersed teams.

Discover new demographics. Some assignments require managers to lead or work with members from different demographic groups: age, ethnicity, gender, nationality. Where geographic crossings involve cultural boundaries by location, demographic crossings often occur in the same location, with members of different cultures. Examples include working in or managing a culturally diverse team, being responsible for organizational diversity initiatives, and mentoring employees of a different culture.

Seek cross-cultural experiences. What roles, assignments, and experiences expose managers to diverse cultures, policy environments, and societal expectations? At the end of the experience, the employees return to their respective offices with a broader perspective and set of skills that they can apply to their work. International business trips, short-term overseas assignments, and routine interaction with teams and individuals from different cultures are all learning opportunities. Global action learning projects are especially powerful ways to prepare managers for global roles.

Cultivate diverse relationships. Learning can take place through cross-cultural relationships. This can take the form of interacting with managers of a different culture in an international assignment or through an organization's intentional effort at cross-cultural pairing. One example is the pairing of expatriate managers with local managers. Through such relationships, managers learn to develop cross-cultural adaptability in working with their counterparts. Within the organization, multicultural work groups are another form of cross-cultural interaction that can facilitate the development of new skills and perspectives.

Benefit: Enhance Your Impact

The true measure of learning is your ability to apply it. To have value, learning must be transferable to different situations and to other people. Experience-based learning can enhance impact. The transfer of learning from experience involves a manager's application of the lessons learned and transmission of new knowledge to other people in the organization.

Stephan, vice president of sales for a midsize pharmaceutical firm, is not an expert in mergers and acquisitions, but he's been through a few during his career. When his company acquires a smaller firm, Stephan is tapped to manage the merging of two sales and marketing operations. He knows he has learned a lot from prior experiences about what to do and what not to do when merging businesses. His challenge is to clarify those lessons, apply them to the current merger, and share them with others in the organization to ease the transition.

Stephan has the opportunity to show a powerful return on his experience in three ways:

- At the *individual* level, the lessons learned are transferred to the context of other work required of the manager. This takes place when a manager can apply the lessons learned from a particular experience to a variety of contexts, from one role to another, or in another organization or culture. Impact is enhanced when the learner abstracts the leadership principles underlying the knowledge being learned.

   Stephan explicitly draws on his prior experience to identify potential pitfalls, the underlying challenges his team members may face, and strategies to minimize problems. He also examines his own leadership style and that of key people in the new department. In doing so, he begins to map out a plan for how he can successfully lead through change.

- At the *group* level, the lessons learned from experience can be transferred to others through conversations in which a group reflects collectively on an experience or when an individual shares the lessons learned from experience with group members. By sharing and practicing new behaviors and skills, managers can transfer the learning they have acquired from experience to other members of their group.

  Stephan knows that his past experience and perspective can be helpful to his peers and to his staff. Informally, he and two colleagues become sounding boards for each other. By talking through their methods, insights, and dilemmas, the three of them magnify their successes and identify trouble spots more quickly. This is particularly helpful because Stephan's boss is "hands-off." He cares about outcomes, not process.

  Stephan is also learning to be open and direct with employees. He acknowledges problems, seeks out feedback, and is clear about his goals for the merged department. As a result, his direct reports know his approach for dealing with change and are similarly applying his tactics.

- At the *organizational* level, the transfer of learning from experience occurs when learning is codified and used to transform general practice. While difficult to achieve, this is the most powerful benefit of experiential learning. As leaders transfer their learning across the organization, they create shortcuts for other leaders to learn the same skills. Unfamiliar skills and behaviors can more rapidly develop in people across the organization, transforming the overall leadership capacity and capability of the enterprise.

Although Stephan is not officially responsible for creating organizational best practices, the relatively smooth integration of the sales and marketing teams has been noticed. Keen on documentation, Stephan has a trove of examples and ideas that he has shared with the human resources team and key executives. With additional acquisitions expected in the coming years, the company hopes to build on his lessons of experience.

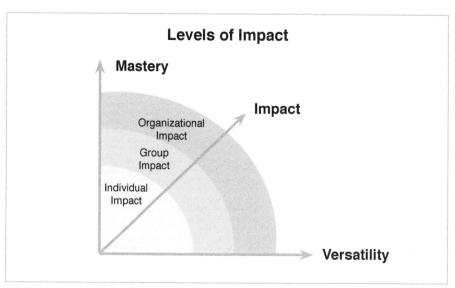

Strategies for Enhancing Impact

The integration of individual experience with systems of transfer can create a cascading impact through the organization, leveraging the investment in learning well beyond a few key people. Three steps are necessary to implement this integrated approach. First, a period of facilitated reflection after the experience allows for the manager to make sense and assimilate what he or she has learned; this helps adaptation and future growth. Second, a just-in-time process of knowledge capture is needed to codify the lessons learned. Third, a method of dissemination is required for the lessons to be communicated across the organization.

Build relationships. Learning is enhanced when developmental experiences and goals have the support of senior management. Support, reflection, sense making, and assimilation of learning are improved through key relationships.

Ideally, Stephan's boss would have supported him in his efforts to apply and extend his knowledge. Fortunately, Stephan had several strong peer relationships and an external mentor. As a manager of others, Stephan was able to do what his boss did not: he invested in relationships to support learning and performance within his department.

Use learning systems. Developmental experiences by themselves are not sufficient to result in organizational impact. Organizations need processes that facilitate the capture and dissemination of lessons learned. In many cases, systems are informal or inconsistent. But even if talent or people management systems aren't in place, you can create your own documentation processes and use them to reach out to the HR function or other managers and executives. Depending on the organization and the nature of your work, you may or may not gain much traction.

For Stephan, a visible success created a platform for sharing information outside his department. The extent to which his lessons learned will be integrated into future merger and acquisition processes will depend primarily on others. Regardless, the transfer of learning into the organization has begun.

Create Your ROE Portfolio

- How do you make your learning visible?
- How do you recognize it for yourself?
- How do you elevate learning to a relevant discussion with others?
- How do you use lessons learned from experience as a point of differentiation between yourself and others?

How? By creating your personal ROE portfolio!

Why a Portfolio?

Work portfolios have been widely used in professional fields such as design, engineering, and the arts. Leaders, too, can create a meaningful portfolio as a way to understand, document, and drive their learning and development.

An architect or designer, for example, puts together a visual portfolio of projects to showcase his skill (mastery) and breadth of experience (versatility). In conversations or proposals, he gives examples, tells stories, and provides client references as a way to show impact. The portfolio serves as a reflection of experience and learning—as a starting point for discussion with others.

The process of putting together a portfolio to show others is also instructive to the professional. It clarifies strengths and differentiators, highlights best practices, and identifies gaps in experience that are important to fill. It can also force thinking about lessons learned and experiences that were valuable—even if the outcomes or processes were less than ideal. For example, the architect could point to a "first" experience—the first time as project manager or the first time he worked with a large-scale project with multiple stakeholders. Perhaps the project missed key deadlines or faced budget shortfalls. These challenges and the management and leadership lessons learned in the process have value that may surface through the portfolio process.

So an ROE portfolio is both a *product* and a learning *process*. It allows you to clarify, track, and communicate experiences of mastery, versatility, and impact. It serves as documentation—ideal for keeping up with today's fast-paced, activity-packed jobs. Just as important, the portfolio process creates space to reflect on learning and demonstrate growth. Creating and maintaining an ROE portfolio can help you grow professionally and, at the same time, serve as a record of your growth.

The portfolio process involves three steps: reflection, portfolio composition, and performance improvement.

Reflection

Before you start planning your future learning opportunities, spend some time understanding how you have learned from experience in the past. Reflect on the questions below. Use a journal to capture your reflections.

- What were key times for learning in your life? Describe situations in which you learned important lessons. How have you used these lessons?

- What experiences have you had that *built* your skills and leadership capacity?

- What experiences have you had that *broadened* your skills and leadership capability?

- What experiences have you had that *benefited* your career, your group, and/or your organization?

Portfolio Composition

The ROE mind-set defines leadership learning as developing experiences that build, broaden, and benefit. By composing your ROE portfolio, you extend the mind-set into a tangible record of learning.

The format of your portfolio is up to you. It can be a simple set of documents or files on your computer, a hard-copy binder or journal, or even a blog or personal Web site. The key is to have something that will be easy to use and maintain. Also give some thought to whether and how you will share your portfolio with others.

Create an overview of your portfolio by listing key experiences and discussing the effect of each experience on your mastery, versatility, and impact. Details, examples, and support materials can be created and included in your portfolio as you wish.

Performance Improvement

To plan how to use your experiences to improve future learning and performance, reflect on the questions below. Use a journal to capture your reflections.

- What are the strategic priorities of the organization?
- What skills and capabilities do I need to learn to be prepared for the next assignment or next level of responsibility?
- What cross-*functional* jobs, tasks, or moves would be important to diversify my experience?
- What cross-*cultural* jobs, tasks, or moves would be important to diversify my experience?
- How could I integrate and/or extend my learning through *relationships*?
- How could I integrate and/or extend my learning through *organizational systems*?

Bringing It Together

Based on your ideas from the previous section, decide on a high-priority learning goal. Use the worksheet on page 26 to state your goal and map out a plan for gaining needed experience.

Planning Worksheet

Development/learning goal:
Time frame:
Assignment, task, role, or move:
Skills, behaviors, actions to practice:
Resources to access:
Relationships to put in place:
Other strategies:

The ROE portfolio is not a static document. Like any portfolio, it can grow and accumulate over time. The steps outlined in this guidebook are only the first. By taking these steps, you have probably gained a better awareness of the experiences that have been most developmental for you—and others where you have learned less, or have not seen the connection and transfer to your current work. In addition, you can also work through your portfolio with a peer or a coach, to jointly reflect and discuss the experience and learning gaps that surface from the process.

By cycling through the reflection, composition, and performance improvement processes, you will be able to create a portfolio that captures important learning experiences. Through the process, you will reinforce the ROE mind-set and begin to frame the lessons you have learned in a clear and compelling way. You can also use your portfolio to guide your performance reviews, leadership development and other goals, and career choices.

Experience Sets You Apart

In their book *The Experience Economy*, Joseph Pine and James Gilmore describe a new economy, one in which experiences are key differentiators. CCL research indicates that the experience economy is real: many managers realize they need important and diverse experiences and are actively seeking out opportunities to set themselves apart.

You know that you cannot wait for a boss, mentor, or HR pro to hand you the right training and learning opportunities. By adopting the ROE mind-set and building your ROE portfolio, you will be able to focus your development and make the most of your lessons of experience. Remember these key points:

1. **Experience may not equal learning.** Learning from experience is important for effective leadership. However, it is not always natural or automatic. Experience becomes valuable when you reflect on the situation, on your behavior and responses, and on what you could do differently to be more effective.

2. **Mastery is valuable.** Use experience to sharpen and shape your expertise and ability to learn from future experiences.

3. **Variety counts too.** Use experience to expand your repertoire of skills and abilities. New experiences force you to adjust your thinking and behavior in some way. A diverse range of experiences extends your professional and emotional bandwidth—allowing you to operate effectively in a broader environment and in a wider area of possibility. You open up to new ways of thinking and acting, and as a result, you are better prepared to address uncertainty.

4. **Consider how to extend the impact.** Of course, you want to be able to apply your lessons of experience to other situations. Also find ways to share your learning—insights, skill, behavior, expertise—with others. You can extend the impact of your learning explicitly through coaching, mentoring, teaching, and discussion, and implicitly through your leadership behavior and effectiveness in achieving goals and desired outcomes. Be open to relationships and processes for extending information and learning broadly through the organization.

5. **Relationships make a difference.** Learning does not take place in a vacuum. Relationships with bosses, mentors, peers, and others are part of the work experience. They can be a source of coaching, feedback, and positive influence—but they can also be draining or get in the way

of your learning and growth. Identify and rely on your supportive relationships and role models—and find ways to work around those who will undermine or stall your efforts.

6. **Develop your ROE portfolio.** Assessments, evaluations, and feedback provide necessary insight into skills, behavior, and performance, but they do so at a specific point in time and within a narrow context. These tools typically ignore or minimize progress and learning over time and through a variety of experiences. An ROE portfolio can help accelerate your development and also strengthen your ability to transfer leadership lessons to others in your organization.

Learning from experience is a continuous, career-long process. The returns on experience are cumulative over time for you and, by extension, for your organization. Rather than treating lessons learned as an afterthought, successful executives develop their sensitivity and ability to harvest critical leadership lessons from experience. By using a return-on-experience framework, you have a systematic, easy-to-implement way to get the learning you need as you spend hours on the job.

Suggested Readings

Berke, D., Kossler, M. E., & Wakefield, M. (2008). *Developing leadership talent*. San Francisco: Pfeiffer.

Berlin, I. (1953). *The hedgehog and the fox: An essay on Tolstoy's view of history*. London: Weidenfeld and Nicolson.

Collins, J. (2001). *Good to great: Why some companies make the leap . . . and others don't*. New York: HarperBusiness.

Dalton, M. A. (1998). *Becoming a more versatile learner.* Greensboro, NC: Center for Creative Leadership.

Lombardo, M., & Eichinger, R. (1989). *Eighty-eight assignments for development in place.* Greensboro, NC: Center for Creative Leadership.

McCall, M. W., Jr., Lombardo, M. M., & Morrison, A. M. (1988). *The lessons of experience: How successful executives develop on the job.* San Francisco: New Lexington Press.

McCauley, C. D. (2006). *Developmental assignments: Creating learning experiences without changing jobs.* Greensboro, NC: Center for Creative Leadership.

Pine, J., & Gilmore, J. (1999). *The experience economy.* Boston: Harvard Business School Press.

Wei, R., & Yip, J. (2008). *Leadership wisdom: Discovering the lessons of experience.* Greensboro, NC: Center for Creative Leadership.

Yip, J., & Wilson, M. (2010). *Learning from experience.* In E. Van Velsor, C. D. McCauley, & M. Ruderman (Eds.), *The Center for Creative Leadership handbook of leadership development* (3rd ed.). San Francisco: Jossey-Bass.

Background

A central question has captivated the interest of researchers and educators at CCL for thirty years: What are the processes by which executives learn, grow, and develop over the course of their careers? To shed light on this question, the Lessons of Experience studies were initiated in the early 1980s. Based on interviews and surveys of 191 senior executives from six large U.S. corporations, CCL researchers gleaned the key developmental events in executives' lives and the lessons learned from those events. In their book, *The Lessons of Experience: How Successful Executives Develop on the Job*

(McCall, Lombardo, & Morrison, 1988), the CCL research team concluded that stretch assignments and developmental relationships were critical to the development of successful executives, more so than the formal training they received.

Across countries, industries, and organizations, the Lessons of Experience studies consistently found more similarities than differences in the types of events that managers say are developmental. In an extension of CCL's earlier research, we identified fifteen types of events that are grouped into five general clusters: challenging assignments, developmental relationships, adverse situations, coursework and training, and personal experience (Yip & Wilson, 2010).

The advice given in this guidebook is drawn from CCL's ongoing research into how leaders learn and develop through experience, as well as educational experience with participants in CCL programs. This guidebook provides a framework for understanding how leadership is developed through experience and suggestions for how leaders can assess and enhance work experience for future development.

Key Point Summary

Nothing teaches leadership like experience. But the benefits of that on-the-job learning opportunity are not guaranteed. To maximize the learning and development potential that lies within work experience, you need a plan. You need to understand what you are gaining from your experience, what is missing, and how to fill any gaps. Using the ROE framework, you actively seek to learn from experience in order to build, broaden, and benefit—that is, to develop your mastery, versatility, and impact.

Mastery is valuable. To increase leadership mastery, the first step is to identify what needs to be learned or improved. You'll want to look at this from two perspectives: the needs of the organization and your own needs. Strategies for building mastery include strategic assignments, job rotations, and action learning projects.

Versatility is important too. Strategies for broadening versatility include working across organizational boundaries of level and hierarchy, horizontal assignments, stakeholder assignments, crossing geographic boundaries, working with people from different demographic groups, seeking cross-cultural experiences, and cultivating diverse relationships.

Consider how to extend the impact of your learning. Apply it to other situations and find ways to share it with others. An integrated approach involves reflection, knowledge capture, and dissemination. Strategies for enhancing impact include building relationships and using learning systems.

Create your ROE portfolio. It allows you to clarify, track, and communicate experiences of mastery, versatility, and impact. The portfolio process creates space to reflect on learning and demonstrate growth. Creating and maintaining an ROE portfolio can help you grow professionally and, at the same time, serve as a record of your growth. The portfolio process involves reflection, portfolio composition, and performance improvement.

By adopting the ROE mind-set and building your ROE portfolio, you will be able to focus your development and make the most of your lessons of experience.

Ordering Information

TO GET MORE INFORMATION, TO ORDER OTHER IDEAS INTO ACTION GUIDEBOOKS, OR TO FIND OUT ABOUT BULK-ORDER DISCOUNTS, PLEASE CONTACT US BY PHONE AT 336-545-2810 OR VISIT OUR ONLINE BOOKSTORE AT WWW.CCL.ORG/GUIDEBOOKS.

CPSIA information can be obtained
at www.ICGtesting.com
Printed in the USA
BVOW11s1954230916
463171BV00006B/41/P